Roger George Clark is a professional broadcaster, photographer and writer. After starting his career in publishing Roger joined the staff of *The Observer* newspaper. Later he moved to the BBC. There he's worked as a producer and broadcaster in news and current affairs, as well as features. Roger has broadcast extensively on local radio, Radio 4 and the BBC World Service.

Running parallel with his publishing and broadcasting careers is a life-long interest in photography. Since his teens Roger has taken tens of thousands of photos at home and abroad.

His pictures have been exhibited at the National Portrait Gallery and are housed in their permanent collection. Roger has had a one-man show at London's National Theatre and the British Library is now acquiring all his photos for their archives.

Besides numerous magazine articles Roger has published six books. *Perfect England* is the fourth to contain his own photos.

Front cover
Brighstone.

Back cover
The *Queen Mary* steams past Cowes.

Following page
The capital of the Island, Newport, seen from the tower of St Thomas's church. Beyond the Guildhall in the centre lies the port and the River Medina leading to Cowes.

PERFECT ENGLAND

The Isle of Wight in the 1960s

Roger George Clark

THE DOVECOTE PRESS

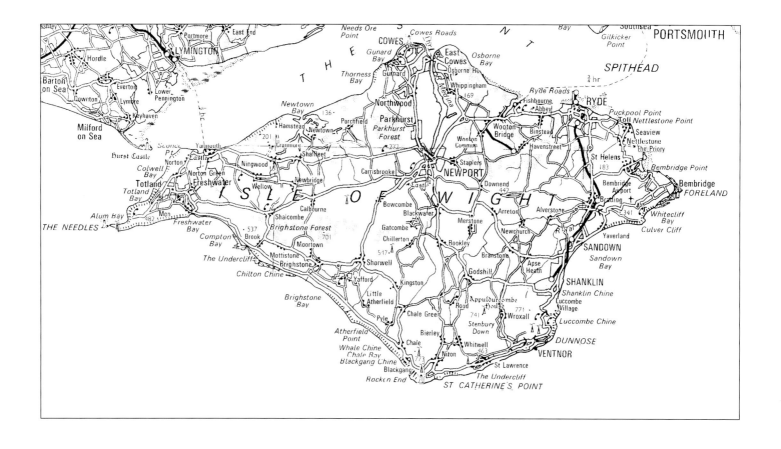

First published in 2008 by The Dovecote Press Ltd
Stanbridge, Wimborne Minster, Dorset BH21 4JD

ISBN 978-1-904-34965-5

© Roger George Clark 2008

Roger George Clark has asserted his rights under the Copyright, Designs
and Patent Act 1988 to be identified as author of this work

Typeset in Monotype Georgia
Printed and bound in Singapore by KHL printing Co . Pte Ltd

A CIP catalogue record for this book is available
from the British Library

Contents

Perfect England

'This is perfect England,' wrote the poet Edward Thomas in 1911. Thomas was writing about the Isle of Wight – standing near the centre of the Island within sight of Carisbrooke Castle. 'It is lovely inland country,' he wrote, 'heaving this way and that with changes now smooth and now sharp . . . Farther away eastward is a great brood of downs, and white clouds round upon round above them, reaching into a cloudless blue dome.'

This was the Isle of Wight I discovered as a teenager over fifty years later when I first came on holiday in 1963. Delighted with what I saw I took a few snapshots with my schoolboy camera and returned the following year. By now I had gone to college and bought myself a more sophisticated camera with a sharp lens. Long before I became a professional broadcaster I contemplated a career as a photographer. The Isle of Wight, I decided, would make an ideal subject for a book. The diamond-shaped island, which was just a couple of miles off England's south coast, was full of intriguing sights to photograph and only 23 miles long and 13 miles wide – small enough for one person to travel around and cover in detail. It was also accessible from my London home and cheap – essential for someone who had to eke out a living on a student grant, and a tiny salary when I found my first employment.

So each year, from 1964 to 1971, I came to the Isle of Wight to take photos. My visits, which lasted a fortnight, usually coincided with Cowes Week. I also paid visits in the spring and returned in the early 1980s.

What brought me to the Island were the great Atlantic liners *Queen Mary* and *Queen Elizabeth* – the largest ships in the world. Their demise was imminent and I wanted to capture them on film before they vanished. Also

The world's largest liner, *Queen Elizabeth*, outward bound for New York.

6

the Royal Yacht *Britannia*, although she survived many years beyond her Sixties' critics. Having photographed these famous ships I turned my camera on the Island.

My companions were a Ward Lock Red Guide and an Ordnance Survey map. The Red Guides were aimed at middle-class holidaymakers. The editor assumed an interest in all things historical – castles, royalty, churches, country houses, monuments, and towns and villages. He poured out information, gratifying the most catholic tastes. It was all here – rambling, yachting, the 'airborne merits' of the climate, beach huts, fishing, the Isle of Wight Hunt (Wednesdays and Saturdays) and that 'old angle of silence' – Yarmouth. If you wanted to find out about 'healing air', early Iron Age culture, paddle-box boats, mystery trips, geology, dinosaurs, Victorian piers, bowls, croquet and billiard-rooms . . . or had an interest in beaches where there were 'no rocks or shingle to trouble the tender-footed' . . . or wanted to attend dinner dances at the Royal Spithead Hotel and Whitecliff Bay Country Club . . . the Red Guide was the book for you. It took me and countless holidaymakers to parts of the Island we never knew existed.

I travelled everywhere by bus or train – £2 a week for a runabout ticket – and walked . . . How I walked! I tramped along endless country roads, roamed over miles of downland, squelched along muddy paths and riverbanks, and pounded the streets of every town and numerous villages. I avoided swimming or paddling in the sea, but explored the beaches and left footprints in the sand. I clambered up church towers and panted almost 800 feet up St Boniface Down, the highest point on the Island. 'We may assure the average stay-at-home citizen, with a short annual holiday, that he will find the ascent, especially on the south side, as stiff a bit of mountaineering as he is likely to care for,' warned the Red Guide. The editor was right. I arrived exhausted at the summit.

The Red Guide also cautioned the wise traveller to avoid standing too near the edge of cliffs. But in a moment of madness I teetered on the brink 200 feet up overlooking Alum Bay and took my photographs. A sudden gust of wind could have hurled me to my doom. But what did I care? When you're young and have a camera in your

St Agnes Church, Freshwater, the only thatched church on the Island.

hands you think you're immortal.

If only I could have stayed in some grand country house – Norris Castle came to mind – or received invitations to dine on board *Britannia* and visit the Royal Yacht Squadron.

Alas, I never mixed in such exalted company. Instead I stayed in a cottage – £12 a week for board and lodging with Mr and Mrs Flux at Byways, Palmers Road, Wootton.

Edward Thomas regarded the Island as 'one of the most civilised corners of the empire' and when I arrived the Isle of Wight still had a strong imperial flavour. You felt it the moment you stepped off the train at the great naval base of Portsmouth, boarded the ferry and steamed across the Solent. Here, with the sun glinting on the water and the wind buffeting your cheeks, you sensed the ghosts of ships past. Before sailing off to war in 1914 the entire British fleet – over 200 warships – paraded before George V. As bands played and flags flew thousands of sailors and marines manned the decks, raising their caps, presenting arms and cheering their distant monarch. For six hours forty miles of naval ships swept past the Royal Yacht *Victoria and Albert*, while aircraft circled overhead. After dark the fleet lit up. 'For miles the waters across to the Isle of Wight were dotted with thousands of

St Boniface Down looms over the Victorian coastal town of Ventnor, which clings to its slopes.

glimmering spots of light', reported *The Times*. The ships resembled 'a floating city of light' and 'the long beams of the searchlights illuminated the sky, mingling with the clouds . . .'

Reality set in when you arrived at Ryde pier. Mind you it was impressive – half a mile long, with steam trains chugging up and down and electric trams purring along the rails. And once you boarded a bus and drove along the sunlit roads it was clear the clichés – 'England in miniature' and 'The Garden Isle' – were true. No wonder over half the Island was declared an Area of Outstanding Natural Beauty. The County Council had no doubt divine intervention was responsible. 'All this beauty is of God', declared the motto beneath their coat of arms.

Here, as the Red Guide promised, were 'warm and smiling valleys . . . trim hedgerows and copses behind which snug farmsteads nestle; and here and there, through gaps in the hills, a glimpse of the sea.' When I found a thatched church at Freshwater my joy was complete.

Critics might carp – it was a classic picture postcard or calendar shot – but to me it encapsulated a vision of fast-fading England.

A wonderful Victorian atmosphere enveloped the Island – hardly surprising since Queen Victoria had lived and died here. In the mid 1840s she and her husband, Prince Albert, built an Italian palace at Osborne, with sweeping views of the Solent. Osborne-style villas sprang up all over the Isle of Wight and spread to the mainland. As you approached the queen's former home or visited the royal church at Whippingham, which like Osborne was partly designed by the Prince Consort, you could feel vibrations in the air – a sensation of slipping back in time to the nineteenth century.

And when Queen Victoria's great-grandson, Admiral of the Fleet, Earl Mountbatten of Burma, became the Island's Governor in 1965, it enhanced the imperial mood. The queen had held him in her arms at his christening. He knew the Island well. His parents were buried in Whippingham churchyard. At the start of the First World War I Mountbatten spent eighteen months as a cadet at Osborne's Royal Naval College. During the Second World War he established at Cowes the headquarters of Britain's ___ __ naval assault group – Force J. This carried ___ _____ ___ __ Dieppe __ 194_ but provided ___ _____ _____ __ ___ ___ of Europe two ____ ____ _____ ___ _____ was created ___ ___ ____ _____ _____ . After the ___ _____ ___ _____ ___tiated India's ___ _____ __ _____ __ ___ _____ng its empire. ___ ____ _____ ___ __ ___ _ Defence Staff. ___ ___ __ _____ ___ __ _____ of Europe's royal ___ ___ _____ __ __gh's uncle and Prince __ ___ _ ___ __ _____ Mountbatten brought glamour to ___ _____ ___s interest was genuine. As Governor he travelle_ ____ d the Island and came over from the mainland seven or eight times each year for the rest of his life, often staying overnight.

'In this Island,' wrote Mountbatten, 'is to be found a pattern of all that is best in England. For the tourist, there are the sandy beaches, the rolling downs and historic buildings . . . For the yachtsmen, the Solent provides

The tourist boat *Saucy Gal* brings holidaymakers ashore during Cowes Week after a trip round the harbour.

what are probably the best sailing waters in the whole country. For the resident, the Island is a haven of peace and quiet in a noisy and bustling world, and yet here the industrialist will find energetic and thriving industries, with skills, enterprise and initiative to match anywhere in the country.'

That was apparent at Cowes where a revolutionary form of amphibious transport, the hovercraft, was developed. Lord Mountbatten was behind it. When the craft's inventor, Christopher Cockerell, failed to find support for his idea in the 1950s he appealed to Mountbatten who was First Sea Lord. The Earl saw its potential, organised help and persuaded Saunders-Roe, in East Cowes, to build a prototype. A new industry developed.

On 24 July 1965 Mountbatten and Christopher Cockerell, launched the world's first regular passenger hovercraft service across the Solent between Ryde and Southsea. The journey took half an hour by conventional ferry. Now you bounced across the water in a breath-taking eight minutes. For the first time passengers could travel directly to and from Ryde by sea without having to trek half a mile to the end of the pier. Large crowds gathered to watch the hovercraft lumbering ashore, spewing spray, shingle and sand. As clouds of débris swirled around me I held my hand over my camera to protect the lens, then whipped my fingers away at the last moment to take my pictures.

But at least the hovercraft came close and filled the viewfinder. Atlantic liners and the Royal Yacht lay miles away. How was I going to photograph them? Others might dash down the Solent in magnificent yachts, or roar across the waters in powerboats. I was an impecunious student. To hire a launch was out of the question and I knew no one who owned so much as a dinghy. Instead I made do with tourist boats, or 'licensed pleasure boats' as the council called them. For 2s 6d (12.5p in modern money) you could take a quick trip round Cowes harbour in the *Saucy Gal*, or *Sally Ann*. Round the liners cost 3s 6d.

There were problems. I had no control over the boat and was hemmed in by holidaymakers. As I struggled to take my pictures excited children waved their arms, leaping up and down in front of me. But at least I was able to come close to the ships. Atlantic liners moved surprisingly fast. One moment they were specks on the horizon, next they loomed over you. The *Queen Mary* and *Queen Elizabeth* came so close you could see the rivets on their hulls. The liners raced past, leaving a huge wash rolling down upon us like liquid mountains, tossing our boat in their wake.

The Atlantic liners were symbols of a bygone age, but they inhabited my imagination. 'Old is beautiful,' was my mantra. What interested me was the past, not the present. While others embraced the 1960s I lived in a time warp. I had no interest in the burgeoning youth culture. I never haunted coffee bars, or went to a gig. I ignored Sixties fashions, music, slang and drugs. Pirate radio, mods and rockers, and the Fab Four were noises off. The nearest I came to groovy events on the Isle of Wight were fly posters on Ryde pier. These publicized the Pink Floyd, the Stack, Amen Corner, and the disc jockey Spike the Mighty Ruler. But they meant nothing to me. Like most people in Britain I was a stick-in-the-mud. But what a world I captured on film!

Idyllic Summers

My photos show an Isle of Wight largely untouched by the Sixties revolution. It was still a place for traditional family holidays. Beatle haircuts were rare. So were T-shirts and jeans. Most people looked as if they'd strolled out of *Picture Post* magazine, or Ealing and Rank Organisation films. Men on holiday wore grey flannels and sports jackets and smoked pipes. Initially I wore my school blazer with leather patches on the elbows. Later I wore a grey suit, white shirt, tie, and black Oxford shoes. Women sported one-piece bathing suits on the beach, seldom bikinis. Grey plastic raincoats were in vogue. Boys wore sandals, or plimsolls. There were no trainers, mountain bikes, mobile phones, walkmen, iPods, Internet, CDs, DVDs, or digital cameras. Indeed, few people carried cameras. Everything was low tech. Fast food meant fish and chips. Chilled drinks were almost impossible to buy outside the large towns.

Nonetheless, there were compensations – a strong community spirit. On 5 August 1965 Lord Mountbatten attended Wootton Church Fête. The week before Queen Elizabeth II, during her first visit to the Isle of Wight since her accession, had installed Mountbatten as the Island's Governor in a grand ceremony at Carisbrooke Castle. When he came to the fête that Thursday afternoon hundreds of people filled the grounds of Wootton Lodge in the High Street. 'As he walked on to the terrace,' reported the *Isle of Wight County Press* newspaper, 'a royal salute was given by the band of the Junior Guardsmen of H.M. Brigade of Guards.'

The fête was an English classic, such as you find in the novels of Agatha Christie (whom Mountbatten admired), or P.G. Wodehouse. Besides the rector, the Rev. A.H. Genower, and the Mayor and Mayoress of Newport, you could see the Chairman of the County Council, assorted military men, JPs, people from local voluntary organisations, Salvation Army women and the broadcaster C.A. Joyce. In short, the great and the good, who sat on chairs in front of the lodge listening to the speeches during the opening ceremony.

'A rosebud buttonhole was presented to Earl Mountbatten by seven-year-old Sheila Featherstone, the rector's grand-daughter,' noted the *County Press*. 'She was rewarded with a kiss from the Earl.' A Girl Guide then handed the distinguished guest a specially bound and inscribed copy of the rector's book *Story of Wootton Church*.

In the course of his speech Mountbatten urged everyone to spend generously. The purpose of the fête, he told them, was to raise money to repair the church.

And spend they did. People swarmed around the stalls snapping up needlework, fancy goods, home-made cakes, fruit, flowers and vegetables. There was a white elephant stall and 'the fishpond – a catch for everybody.' The young guardsmen, looking splendid in their scarlet uniforms, played music throughout the afternoon, including selections from the new musical *Mary Poppins*. Children scampered around, their faces smeared with ice-cream, and visitors enjoyed teas, a buffet, sideshows and a competition – 'Open to all: sixpence a ticket' – top prize £10. Other prizes included a picnic set, a travelling rug, a Sunday dinner at Briddlesford Lodge Farm, a hamper of groceries, a bottle of port and a chicken. Also a mysterious 'compensation prize', presented by the rector. Spend another 6d and you might win the rectory cake.

If you had the good fortune to buy the lucky programme you could win 'Four ten shilling notes issued by the Bank of England.' Meanwhile, the church organist stood by ready to present a crate of beer to the person who won the skittle prize.

As for the book presented to Lord Mountbatten . . . the official programme informed visitors that they, too, could buy a copy: 'The illustrated story of Wootton Church, from 1087 A.D., by the rector (present one) is on sale at the Household Goods Stall, price 2s 6d. Autographed by the author, 1/- extra.'

Mountbatten had time for everyone, chatting amiably with local worthies whom the rector lined up to meet him. Dashing into the crowds he talked informally to old servicemen and, to a family's delight, patted their baby in a pram. He thanked the young guardsmen for their music and took part in raising money.

Earl Mountbatten signs autographs for 2s. 6d. a time at Wootton Church Fête while his A.D.C. collects the money in a tin.

'Earl Mountbatten,' reported the *County Press*, 'accepted an invitation to sign an autograph book and within moments was besieged by dozens of others seeking his signature. The rector then announced that the Earl would sign autographs at 2s 6d a time in aid of the church funds and he was kept busy for some 20 minutes.'

Lord Mountbatten signed over 120 autographs, raising more than £15. Altogether the afternoon's events brought in £380, quite a sum in those days. The local paper said the fête was the most successful ever held in the parish.

The archivist at Wootton Parish Church, Doreen Gazey, caught the atmosphere of those times when she wrote:

'There are many references in the Parish magazines to sunny and warm "Rector's weather" at these events, and none of the fêtes being rained off . . . There were many other social events too. The Harvest Suppers (which took place at the Rafters Holiday Camp) seem to have been very

A young girl presents a buttonhole to the Chancellor of the Exchequer, James Callaghan, as he opens the Carisbrooke Cottage Garden Society summer show in 1965.

During his speech Mr Callaghan said the beauty of the countryside and the peacefulness made the Island one of the most beautiful places anyone could find in the British Isles. With one eye on Britain's ailing economy Mr Callaghan noted that people spending holidays abroad cost the country £360 million a year in foreign exchange. 'But,' asked the Chancellor, 'why go abroad when you can come to the Island?'

Mr Callaghan had a formidable reputation, but this afternoon was at his most relaxed and genial. To be good gardeners, he said, it was necessary to be hard working, patient, philosophical, and have a touch of the gambler, because with this climate they would never garden otherwise. Then they had to wait and hope the results would be fine and good. He considered the Carisbrooke show proved the value of all those qualities.

Mr Callaghan took a considerable time examining the displays and talking to the prize winners. The judges had a difficult task assessing the 1,000 exhibits. There were cups and special awards for everything from fruit and vegetables and flowers, to eggs and handicrafts – hand-knitted hats, mittens, bootees, tea cosies, embroidered tray cloths, paintings and drawings, and 'a map of the Isle of Wight using natural materials.'

Outside the exhibition marquees visitors enjoyed games and sideshows. Adults and children played bingo with bottle tops and caught bouncing balls in baskets on sticks. Mr Callaghan wandered among the crowds, chatting to anyone who came up to him, pausing to sign an autograph for a disabled old lady in a wheelchair and cheerfully signing his name on a scrap of paper for a teenager. Security was light in those days – just a few policemen keeping a discreet eye on things in the background.

The Carisbrooke Show, like the Wootton Church Fête and countless other events throughout the Island, epitomised traditional English life. Only in Cowes did I notice a hint of modernity. There you might see a few girls in mini skirts and yachtsmen in up-to-date sports clothes. These were mostly people who came over from the mainland, or abroad. They were here for the sailing and brought a more stylish dress sense with them.

popular. The Parish Magazine for November 1959 records that 140 guests consumed 65½ lbs of pork, 17 pheasants, 5 gallons of cider and 5 gallons of beer, besides apple pies, cheese, trifles, minerals and tea . . . '

The number of guests was limited to 160 in succeeding years, such was the demand for tickets which, in 1967, cost 5/- (or 25p).

The children of the parish did well, too, attending anything up to six Christmas parties. Then there were the Sunday school outings. One year the church needed three coaches to transport all the youngsters.

A few weeks after Lord Mountbatten visited Wootton Church Fête the Chancellor of the Exchequer, James Callaghan, opened the annual summer show organised by the Carisbrooke Cottage Garden Society. Callaghan, who later became Britain's prime minister, owned a farm on the mainland and had a genuine knowledge of agriculture. He, too, was charmed by the Isle of Wight.

Royal Cowes

Cowes Castle, headquarters of the Royal Yacht Squadron.

During Cowes Week, held at the beginning of August, the world seemed to descend on the little coastal town. What began as a small nineteenth century regatta rapidly grew into an international event transforming Cowes into the greatest yachting port in Britain. The first regatta, or parade of sail, was held in 1814. This led to the establishment of the earliest yachting club for aristocrats in the summer of the following year. The club eventually became the Royal Yacht Squadron occupying Cowes Castle – one of Henry VIII's coastal defences built in 1539. The club was so exclusive that it black-balled Lord Mountbatten for years, though he became a member in 1943.

The climax was the Edwardian era. On one occasion before the First World War five monarchs attended the regatta. The German Kaiser, Wilhelm II, was a regular competitor. And in 1909 the last Tsar, Nicholas II, came on

A Royal Yacht Squadron official follows a race through his telescope.

a State visit, spending four days at Cowes on his fabulous steam yacht, *Standart*. A few years later he and his family were murdered during the Russian Revolution,

Cowes Week was still royal when I went there and remained so for many years. In 1967 yachtsmen from 15 nations took part in the racing. As *Britannia* arrived at her moorings one of the guard ships, *HMS Carysfort*, fired a 21-gun salute, the sound echoing around the town. All the ships and clubs were dressed overall in honour of the royal visit, as were many of the yachts.

Thousands of spectators, some armed with telescopes, lined the waterfront each day gazing at nearly 400 craft competing in the racing. Somewhere out there on the crowded water, amid a forest of masts, they could glimpse the Duke of Edinburgh sailing the royal yawl *Bloodhound*, or his Flying Fifteen *Coweslip*. With him were Prince Charles and Princess Anne. Vast crowds gathered on the Victoria Parade and near the Royal Yacht Squadron steps hoping to see the Duke. 'The crowds swept forward as Prince Philip stepped ashore, after waiting as long as two hours to catch a glimpse of him,' reported the *County Press*. 'Prince Philip acknowledged their welcome with a smile before leaving the steps and entering the castle.'

Cowes Week was always a brilliant social occasion – as much about balls and parties as about racing – and 1967 was no exception. Prince Philip held a private dinner party on board *Britannia* attended by Earl Mountbatten, who spent the night on board the royal yacht. There were parties everywhere and a grand ball at the Royal London Yacht Club. The lawns of Northwood House were covered with marquees inside which the club created a glorious fantasy. The largest marquee, which was 200 feet long, contained a gold and orange carousel stretching up to the ceiling decorated with sea horses, dolphins and fairy lights. A backcloth, portraying fairgrounds and mermaids swimming in a shadowy underwater world, extended along the whole length of the ballroom. Red candles flickered in wine bottles on every table as 14 members in the royal party mingled with 800 guests.

One of the great characters in those days was the yacht designer, Uffa Fox, who lived on the Island. 'He loved good food and wine, the latter sometimes a little too much,' remembered the former prime minister, Edward Heath, an accomplished yachtsmen who frequently stayed in Cowes in the 1960s and '70s. 'His ebullient nature displayed itself both in a jovial heartiness and in an explosive temper which at times he found difficult to control.' At dinner parties Uffa would launch into sea-shanties and his uninhibited behaviour shocked some people. Back in the 1950s he fell off his horse and broke his ankle. 'He promptly ordered up a sedan chair and set out daily to tour the pubs like a Roman emperor, borne by two sturdy porters and accompanied by an umbrella-toting neighbour,' reported the American magazine *Time*.

Uffa Fox was a boon companion and helmsman to the Duke of Edinburgh. It was he who designed the Flying Fifteen *Coweslip* – a wedding present for the Queen and the Duke from the people of Cowes. In 1967 Uffa invited Prince Philip to a dinner party in his home overlooking the harbour. On the menu was a 25lb salmon caught in the Solent. This was served to the Duke, Prince Charles and Princess Anne. The fish was so big Uffa sought the help of a famous firm of marine engineers, yacht fitters and chandlers in the High Street. 'The fish,' the *County Press* informed readers, 'was 44 inches long and a specially large copper kettle was hurriedly made by Messrs. Pascall Atkey, Ltd., in which to cook it. An equally large wooden platter was made to serve the giant salmon.'

Like most holidaymakers I could only read about these events in newspapers, or magazines. I never set eyes on the royals, or celebrities, but you sensed they were there. Nonetheless, there was plenty to see and photograph. And everyone could enjoy the firework display at the end of the week. As I rested my camera on a railing overlooking the harbour, rockets exploded over the town and twinkling stars and coloured lights reflected in the shimmering waters.

But not everyone was pleased. The yachting correspondent of *The Times*, John Young, seemed immune to the charms of the regatta. He thought the Solent 'far from ideal sailing' and Cowes 'a dull little town'. He disapproved of the 'stuffiness' and 'the white-capped, blue-blazered figures' in the Royal Yacht Squadron. 'The wind of change is still no more than the merest zephyr,' he complained.

Echoes from the Past

Doubtless, John Young would have disapproved of the capital Newport, which lay five miles to the south of Cowes, in the heart of the Island. This sturdy market town is the only major town that lies away from the coast. Historically it dates from Roman times nearly 2,000 years ago. You can see the remains of a Roman villa in Cypress Road. The town grew up because it was close to Carisbrooke Castle. Much of it was, and is, unspoilt. Many historic buildings survive, including the Grammar School founded in 1614. Here Charles I stayed in 1648 whilst on parole from Carisbrooke Castle. The following year he was executed in London. The architect John Nash, who designed Buckingham Palace, built the Guildhall and the County Club. In addition there were two fine parish churches – I took pictures from the top of St Thomas's tower – Georgian houses and small Victorian shops. Hidden away on the outskirts was the port. Few visitors came here, but I was fascinated by the melancholy beauty of the old industrial buildings and the coasters and barges tied up on the quay.

A railway viaduct crossed the harbour leading to Newport Station. Had I known that steam trains were soon to disappear after I first came to the Island I would have taken more pictures. As it was I had to make do photographing a derelict station, some smashed locomotives and a tank engine awaiting destruction.

Apart from Newport all the main towns – Yarmouth, Cowes and Ryde – were originally built in the north of the Island. 'The worship of the sea and nature in the raw, where it faces the Channel, is at its earliest a late-Georgian cult', observed the poet John Betjeman in a 1949 radio talk. 'The old idea was to put your house as far away from wind and sun as you could.' Invaders also threatened the Island. After the Romans came the Jutes, Saxons and Danes until the Norman conquest in 1066. Later the French and Spanish. Local people watched the Armada sail past in 1588. And during the summer of 1625, while haymaking was taking place, pirates from North Africa landed and kidnapped the Island men and women. It was

Shanklin's most famous attraction – the Chine. The tree-lined gorge, which is 300 feet wide at its mouth and 150 feet deep, was carved out of the rock by a tiny stream. The chine played a vital role in the Second World War when PLUTO – the Pipe Line Under The Ocean – ran down the ravine piping fuel to the Normany beaches after the 1944 invasion.

safer for the inhabitants to face the mainland.

Big changes came, however, in the nineteenth century. People took notice when the eminent physician Sir James Clark, who later became Queen Victoria's doctor, endorsed the health-giving properties of Ventnor's climate. 'Nothing along the south coast will bear comparison with it,' he enthused. Queen Victoria's presence at Osborne provided the ultimate accolade. The middle-classes flocked to the Isle of Wight. Steam packets across the Solent made the journey easier and soon railway lines were criss-crossing the Island. Along the south-east coast three small villages, which were little more than clusters of fishermen's cottages, grew into major coastal resorts. Within five miles you could find Ventnor, Shanklin and Sandown. All

had gorgeous beaches overlooking the English Channel.

John Keats was one of the early discoverers of the Island. While staying at Castle Road, Carisbrooke, in 1817 the poet penned the opening lines of *Endymion* – 'A thing of Beauty is a joy forever.' Like Edward Thomas a century later Keats relished the landscape in the middle of the Island. 'I see Carisbrooke Castle from my window,' he wrote, 'and have found several delightful wood-alleys, and copses, and quick freshes.'

Two years later in July 1819 he stayed at Shanklin. 'I am now,' he wrote to his love Fanny Brawne, 'at a very pleasant cottage window, looking on to a beautiful hilly country, with a glimpse of the sea . . . ' He enjoyed wandering along the coast as far as Steephill and admired the 'wondrous chine.' When I went there in the 1960s it was still wondrous, although a popular tourist attraction for decades. Sunlight filtered through the trees. Rare ferns and plants abounded. It was difficult to imagine the tiny stream that tumbled over the cliff had carved out this deep valley in the rock. Difficult also to imagine that in the Second World War marine commandoes had carried out exercises here before raiding Dieppe. Afterwards came PLUTO – the Pipeline Under The Ocean – another of Lord Mountbatten's ideas. This ran from the Island to Normandy, supplying the allied invasion forces with fuel after the D-Day landings in 1944. You could still see some of the pipes running down the chine.

A couple of miles away in Bonchurch stood the Winterbourne Hotel, a large country house on a steep hill overlooking the sea. It was once rented by Charles Dickens. Here, in 1849, he wrote part of his autobiographical novel *David Copperfield*. The author was delighted with Bonchurch – 'cool, airy, private bathing, everything delicious – I think it is the prettiest place I ever saw in my life, at home or abroad.' Each day he worked on his novel in one of the first-floor rooms overlooking the garden and the sea. Then he would stride up St Boniface Down: 'It makes a great difference in the climate to get a blow there and come down again.'

Dickens's sons played with 'the golden haired lad of the Swinburnes.' Algernon Swinburne lived further up the Hill at East Dene and later made a name for himself as a critic and poet. 'No one,' wrote John Betjeman, 'made the sea hiss and clang in English poetry better than he.' Although Swinburne spent much of his life in London he was buried in Bonchurch in 1909.

During the nineteenth century the Isle of Wight attracted some of the most intelligent and controversial people of the day.

The English naturalist Charles Darwin, who formulated the theory of evolution by natural selection, began writing his revolutionary book *On the Origin of Species* in Sandown in 1858. He thought the village was 'the nicest seaside place which we've ever seen.'

The Russian author Ivan Turgenev sketched out the characters for his masterpiece *Fathers and Sons* during a three-week holiday in Ventnor in August 1860.

For almost 40 years that 'tall, swarthy, Spanish-looking man with an eye like a sword' – the poet Alfred, Lord Tennyson – lived in Farringford House near Freshwater Bay. Some his best-known poems, *The Charge of the Light Brigade, Enoch Arden* and *Maud*, as well as most of *Idylls of the King,* were written on the Island. And the crown of his life's work, *Crossing the Bar*, was scribbled down in a few minutes while travelling on the ferry from Lymington to Yarmouth.

As Poet Laureate Tennyson enjoyed a status similar to a modern celebrity. Famous people came out to Freshwater to meet him. They included the Prince Consort, the author of the *Alice* books Lewis Carroll, the Italian patriot Garibaldi, as well as Edward Lear and Charles Kingsley. Charles Darwin came over and the actresses Ellen Terry and Jenny Lind dropped in, as did the composers Arthur Sullivan and Hubert Parry, and the painters Millais and G.F. Watts. Tennyson was mobbed when he appeared in public and plagued by sight-seers at home. People climbed trees and peered in at his windows in a hope of seeing the famous poet. Much of Tennyson's life was spent out of doors and his favourite walk was along the Downs to the Needles. To escape prying eyes he would run across the wooden bridge built over a muddy lane at the end of his garden, cape flying, hat crammed down over his face, and make his way up onto the High Down with its staggering views of the sea. Here he was frequently harassed by autograph-hunters. He once fled from a flock of sheep having mistaken them for admirers. When the poet died a 38-foot high cross, carved from Cornish granite, was erected at the summit and the Down named after him.

Near to Farringford lay Dimbola Lodge. Here lived the photographer Julia Margaret Cameron who invented the close-up portrait. Her reputation has risen over the decades, but when I went to Yarmouth in the 1960s you could see some of her photos on display in a waiting-room at the end of the wooden pier. Once people realised their value they were removed and placed in a proper archive and safely conserved.

There was no knowing who might arrive in the Island next. Even Karl Marx came three times to try to improve his health – first to Ryde in 1874, then Ventnor in 1881. Some people might have thought that the founder of modern communism, who so despised bourgeois society, would have disliked the conservative Isle of Wight. But no. It's 'a little paradise,' he wrote to his friend and philosopher Friedrich Engels. Marx puffed his way up to the summit of St Boniface Down where now, in the 1960s, I found a radar station. During the Second World War RAF Ventnor had played a vital role in Britain's radar defences and was attacked by German bombers. But it was soon back in action and still operating in a more peaceful world.

A slight shift in dates and Karl Marx might have encountered the young Winston Churchill. He came to the Island as a child. In 1878 Churchill spent part of his summer holidays in Ventnor and returned the following year. 'I loved Ventnor,' Churchill wrote later in life. He was taken for long walks over the Downs and through the Undercliff, a spectacular series of broken terraces up to half a mile wide created by landslides. These stretch six miles from St Catherine's to Bonchurch. Tumbled rocks, trees and dense undergrowth hem in a twisting coastal road bounded by towering cliffs.

One day, while walking along those cliffs, Churchill had an alarming experience: 'We saw a great splendid ship with all the sails set, passing the shore only a mile or two away.' It was the training ship *Eurydice*. All of a sudden black clouds filled the sky. A storm blew up with heavy gusts of wind and blinding falls of snow. Churchill was hurried home. The next time he went out on the cliffs there was no splendid ship in full sail, just three black masts sticking out of the water. The *Eurydice* had capsized in the storm and gone to the bottom taking over 300 young sailors to their deaths. Divers went down to bring up the corpses. Churchill was horrified: 'I was told – and it left a scar on my mind – that some of the divers had fainted with terror at seeing the fish eating the bodies . . .'

This disaster was one of many that have given the Isle of Wight's southern coast, or the Back of the Island as it's known, such a sinister reputation. Exposed to the full force of the English Channel gales it is dangerous for shipping. Chale Bay, or the Bay of Death as it was dramatically entitled in earlier times, is notorious. More than a dozen vessels were wrecked here one night in 1757. The medieval lighthouse built on the summit of St Catherine's Hill was useless. The light was too high, feeble and invisible in foul weather. It was only after the disastrous loss of the *Clarendon* in 1836 that a new lighthouse was constructed half a mile away hard by the shore.

The American novelist Henry James was fortunate to find the southern coast in a more genial mood when he arrived on a short visit in 1878. Although he grumbled about the railway that brought him from Ryde – 'detestable . . . a gross impertinence' – his temper improved once he reached Ventnor. The little town clinging to the side of a steep hill reminded James of 'one of the bright-faced towns that look down upon the Mediterranean.' And he was charmed by Bonchurch. 'Delicious . . . It is like a model village.' The Undercliff was 'the prettiest place in the world . . . It is impossible to imagine anything more charming than this long, blooming platform, protected from the north by huge green bluffs and plunging on the other side into the murmuring tides.'

Edward Elgar, the English composer, was also enchanted with the Back of the Island. He spent his honeymoon in a house overlooking the sea at Ventnor in 1889. Elgar and his new bride Alice rode out to Freshwater in a horse-driven coach. 'Cave and arched rocks', noted the composer in his diary. 'Had a wade: kissed her wet foot.'

But who cared about Elgar in the 1960s? Or the Isle of Wight? This was the age of rock 'n' roll, satire and mockery, the Profumo scandal, James Bond and student protests – revolution even. What chance had the composer of *Land of Hope and Glory*, or an island steeped in Victoriana? Suggestions that I was holidaying there and, worse still, taking photographs were greeted with condescending smiles and ironic remarks from my mainland friends. Perhaps if they had known about Karl Marx they would have been less patronising.

Or D.H. Lawrence whose controversial *Lady Chatterley's Lover*, banned for years, was at last being published. His visit to Freshwater in 1909 stirred him to write his second novel, *The Trespasser*, about adultery and a doomed love affair. Large parts of the novel are set in the Isle of Wight. Interspersed with lyrical descriptions of the Island, and red-hot but ill-fated love-making, are numerous references to the composer Richard Wagner whom the hero and heroine adore. To them the Island is 'Sieglinde's island.' The sound of the foghorn on the Needles lighthouse resembles 'the call of the horn across the sea to Tristan.' Barking sheepdogs remind them of the giants in the *Ring of the Nibelung*. 'The rippling sunlight on the sea was the Rhine maidens spreading their bright hair to the sun.' According to one critic the novel is 'unbelievably bad', but Lawrence was right about the Wagnerian atmosphere. When the mist descends, or the rugged coast is lashed by storms, there it is. The Bay of Death would provide a fitting graveyard for the *Flying Dutchman*.

Or what about Auden and Isherwood? Surely their presence would have lent a radical respectability to the Isle of Wight. The two poets had stayed at Freshwater when they were students in 1926 and Isherwood later returned. As he stood high up on Tennyson Down close to the granite cross, surveying the sparkling sea and sweep of the Island, Isherwood said to himself, 'I am happy.'

But these musings meant little to most people in 1960s Britain. To them the Isle of Wight was the ultimate in uncool – until the American singer, composer and poet Bob Dylan arrived for the 1969 August Bank Holiday Festival of Music. D-Day, someone called it.

Pop Festival Invasions

A small pop concert had been staged on two trailers the previous year near Godshill. About 9,000 people came. Now the organisers planned something much larger in the green fields of Wootton. The festival was held close to Mr and Mrs Flux's cottage and the lodge where I had photographed Lord Mountbatten attending the church fête.

'Help Bob Dylan sink the Isle of Wight on August 31st,' urged the adverts. Thousands nearly did. The Island's population suddenly doubled and there was no way local people could cope with the invasion. For three days 150,000 fans sang and danced. Road surfaces turned to dust with the pounding of thousands of feet. Free love, flower power and mind-bending drugs thrived.

'Thousands of fans cheered as a naked girl danced in front of the stage, wearing only a red bandanna and with red paint on her arms and nose,' reported *The Observer* newspaper. 'The cheers grew louder as the girl, who was very attractive, bounded into the press enclosure and turned cartwheels and somersaults. She was circled by photographers as she danced for ten minutes, writhing on the ground . . .'

Dylan turned up three hours late on Sunday night. It was his first major public performance since his motorcycle accident in 1966. 'In the cool evening air, as evident as the sweet odour of marijuana, hung an almost palpable yearning for some transcendent experience', *Time* magazine noted. 'When he came on, he was greeted by applause that sounded like the roar of surf from the nearby Channel.'

Among the audience were John Lennon, Yoko Ono, Ringo Star, George Harrison, Keith Richards, Bill Wyman, Elton John, and the actress Jane Fonda. The pop messiah sang for 70 minutes and spoke only a few sentences to his adoring fans. 'All told, he sang 17 songs, including two encores, and then hopped into a waiting car behind the stage and zoomed away into the darkness,' reported *Time*.

The national press thought the festival was fun – a story of peace and love. But local people found it frightening. 'What Price Pop?' thundered the *County Press*. The

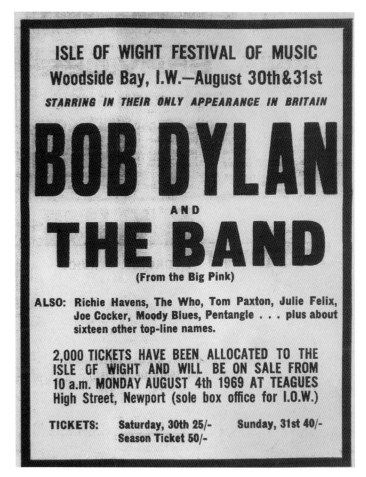

Newspaper advert for the 1969 Wootton pop festival starring Bob Dylan.

paper's editorial 'despaired of human beings who could leave such an indescribable scene of litter and filth behind them.' It was 'shocked by the remains of fires on graves in the nearby graveyard,' and 'concerned by the fears of residents for the safety of their property.'

As I knew Wootton well I joined the chorus of protests. Writing to the local paper I condemned the festival and demanded to know who was going to pay to clear up the mess. And, like many people, I predicted worse trouble if something similar took place in future.

Riots broke out next year. The 1970 pop festival, which was held at Tennyson's Freshwater, was even bigger and lasted five days. About 600,000 people came. And no wonder. The programme was packed with legendary figures, including The Who, Moody Blues, Procul Harum, The Doors, Miles Davis, Joan Baez, Jethro Tull, Donovan, Kris Kristofferson, Joni Mitchell and many more. The festival was larger than Glastonbury and Live Aid combined. Jimi Hendrix was the major star. Within a month he'd died from drink and drugs.

Anarchists mingled with the crowds. So did Hell's Angels. Punch-ups followed. Local shops ran short of food. Hippies, high on drugs, swamped the countryside and crammed the buses. Thousands indulged in nude bathing in Compton Bay. 'At one stage, hippies were queuing to get down to the beach and our photographer was the only man with his trousers on,' reported the *County Press*.

A Lost World

Was this 'perfect England'? Some people thought it was. The Isle of Wight festivals were defining moments in British culture – landmarks for a generation. But I avoided them and concentrated on what interested me. When I took these photos the great Cunard liners still plied across the Atlantic to New York. *Britannia* graced Cowes Week. Paddle steamers thrashed across the Solent. That grey monster, the Saunders-Roe Princess flying boat, lay mothballed on a slipway in East Cowes. And the Island had a governor. All have now gone.

Cowes is losing its charm. Corporate hospitality tents litter the Victoria Parade in Cowes Week. So do their adverts. Has the event, I wonder, become too big – just another bloated international sporting occasion that's losing its character?

Close to the Royal Yacht Squadron you can now find a marina. Metal gangways lead down from the shore onto a floating pontoon running parallel with the Victoria Parade. Motor cruisers clutter the harbour.

Modern architects are erecting Costa del Sol-style buildings overlooking the waterfront. Perhaps that yachting correspondent in *The Times* who wanted the wind of change to blow through Cowes would approve. But where's the elegance?

Car and passenger ferries have changed, as has the hovercraft. Steam trains no longer rattle along Ryde pier, or across the countryside – except for one heritage line. Storms smashed Shanklin and Ventnor piers and waves destroyed the Arched Rock at Freshwater. Modern lamps have spoilt Yarmouth pier. A helicopter-landing pad was dumped on top of the Needles lighthouse. Newport's railway bridge and viaduct were knocked down and the harbour devastated by a concrete roadway on stilts. What remained of the East Medina tide mill disappeared. The wrecked paddle steamer *Medway Queen* was towed away to the mainland. The Bristol double-decker buses on which I travelled so many miles around the island were scrapped, or ended their days in a transport museum. And Wootton Lodge, where Lord Mountbatten attended the church fête, has gone, replaced by modern houses.

Another casualty was Steephill Castle in the south of the Island. Built in the 1820s, the castle was the principal mansion in Ventnor. Sir Joseph Paxton, who designed the Crystal Palace for the 1851 Great Exhibition, was enchanted by it. 'I have visited nearly every place of note from Stockholm to Constantinople', he wrote, 'but never have I seen anything more beautiful than this.' Steephill Castle was pulled down in 1964.

I missed East Cowes Castle, too, which John Nash built for himself in a commanding position overlooking the Solent. The artist J.M.W. Turner stayed as a guest in the summer of 1827. Entranced by this Gothic fantasy he dashed off sixty sketches, as well as paintings of the newly established Cowes Regatta, with the castle in the foreground. But in the 1960s few people cared about Gothic architecture. Modernism was king. East Cowes Castle was demolished and a housing estate built in its place.

And few people on the Island cared about Turner. The art critic and historian Kenneth Clark might consider him 'a genius of the first order – far the greatest painter England has ever produced.' But you could search island books in vain, scour public libraries and examine all the publicity and tourist literature and find little about him. Yet during that visit in 1827, and earlier in the summer of 1795 when Turner had travelled all over the Island, the artist had produced a remarkable series of sketches and paintings. Wherever I went I was following in Turner's footsteps.

Sifting through my photos decades later I realised I had walked along the same coastal path where Turner had wandered and visited the same churches, villages and towns. In a couple of instances – Bembridge windmill and Freshwater Bay – I had taken my photos from the same angles Turner had chosen 170 years before.

The Isle of Wight looked small on a map, but seemed enormous when you relied on public transport and had to walk. As a result the Island took longer to photograph than I anticipated. Architectural and landscape photography proved difficult. I wanted sunlight to add sparkle to my pictures and cloud-filled skies. Nature was capricious and I had to return to my subjects many times to ensure the best results. By the time I'd assembled a good collection of pictures other books had appeared and no one was interested in my photos. I joined the BBC and broadcasting took over from photography. I returned to the Island from time to time, however, as my parents had moved to Cowes.

The last time I took photos on the Island was in summer of 1981. Back in 1969 I had the good fortune to go out on the water with the famous marine photographer Keith Beken. 'The old yachts and some of the new have more curves than a woman', he told me as we slammed across the Solent in his high-speed launch. 'You must accentuate them.' Now, years later, I met Keith again and his son Kenneth, who had followed in his father's footsteps. Established in 1839 Beken of Cowes had a worldwide reputation. They were by appointment to Queen Victoria, King George V and the Duke of Edinburgh. Prince Philip claimed he had an unjustified reputation for disliking photographers, but he welcomed the Beken camera. On one occasion Keith towed the Duke and Uffa Fox home when their Flying Fifteen nearly sank.

I had also heard that Edward Heath was going to appear at Cowes. The former prime minister had won the Round-the-Island Race four times in his yachts *Morning Cloud*, three of them in consecutive years in the early 1970s. Saturday 8 August 1981 saw the start of the Fastnet Race

The former prime minister, Edward Heath, sets out from Cowes in 1981 to watch the start of the Fastnet Race. Mr Heath's yachts won the Round-the-Island race four times.

– a gruelling five-day contest that began at Cowes, ran to the Fastnet Rock off southern Ireland and back to the finish at Plymouth.

Walking down onto the pontoons in the harbour I could see the large, expensive yachts that were going to take part in the race. The pontoons heaved up and down in the swell, vibrating when people ran across them. I'd just taken a picture when Edward Heath quietly appeared through the crowds. He was alone and wearing a Cambridge blue cardigan with the name *Morning Cloud* embroidered in white over his heart. His hair was white, too, but he looked brown and fit, though a little overweight. I took a few pictures from a distance while Mr Heath waited to go on board a white cabin cruiser. Occasionally he exchanged a few words with one or two yachtsmen. At other times he stood silent, lost in thought.

Suddenly, the pontoon on which we were standing tilted at an alarming angle. Up and up and up it went. For a moment it seemed as if we might capsize and be thrown into the water. Stepping back sharply, I leapt onto a neighbouring pontoon. The weighty Mr Heath slowly shifted himself to the rising side as did many others. The pontoon gently righted itself and people laughed nervously. But Mr Heath remained impassive and behaved as if nothing had happened. Not a flicker of an expression. After a few minutes he clambered over the railings of a yacht, made his way onto a second boat, then boarded the white motor cruiser. Making his way up onto the flying bridge he sat down, watching the activity in the harbour as the Fastnet Race crews prepared to leave. On board were some beautiful young women. He exchanged a few words with them, but otherwise remained absorbed by the yachting and his own thoughts – a lonely, isolated man.

Well might he look concerned. Two years before disaster had overtaken the race. A freak storm hit the competitors. Dozens of yachts were lost and 15 people drowned. One of the few boats to reach the finish was Mr Heath's. 'It was the worst experience I have ever had,' he said after the ordeal. 'It was a raging sea with enormous waves and one of them picked us up and laid us on our side.'

As the motor cruiser glided away amongst the racing yachts I photographed Mr Heath in profile. Soon he was lost from sight. This was one of the last pictures I took on the Island. In future I would turn my cameras on other subjects and pursue my broadcasting career. Curiously enough the Island was responsible for that. In 1897 the Italian physicist and inventor, Guglielmo Marconi, came to Alum Bay. There he set up what he called the world's 'first permanent wireless station'. Later he moved the equipment to Niton, overlooking the English Channel, and carried out more experiments. Without Marconi there would have been no radio and I would never have become a broadcaster.

I put away my Island pictures and forgot about them. Nearly forty years later I rediscovered the negatives. Some were neatly filed in brown paper envelopes. Others had gathered dust in a tin. As I looked through my pictures I was filled with nostalgia. The photos carried an emotional punch. They were taken from a point of view long out of favour, but prevalent then. Here was the lost world of my youth – joyful interpretations of Island life –

an English way of life now under threat on the mainland. They showed the Island as it was – when you could stand on the beach at Ryde, or the Victoria Parade at Cowes, and gaze at the Atlantic liners gliding by. Or wander down to Fishbourne, as I did one evening, and watch the *Queen Mary* miles away on the horizon steaming into the sunset, while ripples from her wash lapped around my feet.

And yet, despite changes, much of the Island I so admired when young is still there. Queen Victoria's Osborne House looks more splendid than ever. The monks still pursue their devotions at Quarr Abbey. Small shops still thrive in many towns and villages. Flour is still ground at Calbourne water mill. And much of the landscape is intact. When John Betjeman came to Freshwater in 1949 and strode up onto Tennyson's Down he found the walk towards the Needles 'like a thrilling and terrifying dream . . . Probably this south western coast of Wight is the longest stretch of unspoiled and colossal landscape in the south-west of England.' That was true half a century later.

'A sense of separateness still lingers', observed the travel writer Sara Wheeler when she journeyed round the Island in 2001. It was 'a curiously old-fashioned backwater replete with 19th-century houses and quaint tearooms . . . a quiet haven in unquiet times.'

A ferry skipper caught the mood when he told his passengers, 'We will shortly be arriving at the Isle of Wight. Please put your watches back 50 years.'

Roger George Clark
October 2008

Opposite page For over 40 years the Royal Yacht *Britannia* graced Cowes Week. The Duke of Edinburgh, the Prince of Wales and Princess Anne often took part in the racing and entertained and slept on board. Holidaymakers, hoping to catch a glimpse of royalty, took trips round the royal yacht. The middle flag indicates the Duke of Edinburgh is on board. The union flag at the fore shows that he is an Admiral of the Fleet and the Trinity House flag at the mizzen indicates that he is the Master of Trinity House. The Trinity House Jack is also associated with the Prince of Wales.

Royal Cowes

Above People from all over the world throng the narrow, winding High Street during Cowes Week. It's the main shopping thoroughfare and many 18th- and 19th- century buildings still exist.

Right The fashionably attired mingle with ordinary islanders as they pass the florist and fruiterers K.W. Franks in Cowes High Street.

Opposite page The yacht *Dolphin*, built in 1909, drifts down to the mouth of the River Medina at Cowes. The town, which is at the northern tip of the Island overlooking the Solent, is divided in two by the river – Cowes on the left, East Cowes on the right. When Henry VIII ordered the building of two 'Cowes' – or forts – in 1539 on either side of the estuary, as part of improvements to coastal defences, he began the development of the port. This later became one of the world's leading yachting centres.

Above Watched by curious spectators a TV news cameraman records the scene from the Victoria Parade during Cowes Week.

Below Press photographers, hoping to photograph sailing celebrities, wait to go afloat from the Victoria Parade.

Above A BBC television outside broadcast unit prepares to go on the air on the bastion of the Royal Yacht Squadron during Cowes Week. Behind them are the 22 brass cannon that once belonged to the *Royal Adelaide*. The guns signal the start and finish of yacht races and fire salutes.

Opposite page top Yachtsmen embark from the Victoria Parade. In the background is Cowes Castle. Originally built as a harbour fort by Henry VIII in 1539 it is now the headquarters of the Royal Yacht Squadron.

Opposite page bottom left Standing on the battlements of Cowes Castle two members of the Royal Yacht Squadron's Sailing Committee observe the finish of a yacht race. The official with binoculars calls out the numbers while the other identifies the yachts and notes down the order in which they cross the line.

Opposite page bottom right Solent Sunbeams cross the Royal Yacht Squadron starting line during the 1965 Cowes Week. This classic keel boat was designed in the 1920s. The American destroyer *USS Brownson*, which was on a goodwill trip to Europe, keeps guard.

A contrast in styles!

Left All aboard the *Sally Ann.* For 2s 6d (12½p) she whisked holidaymakers round Cowes harbour for twenty minutes to watch the yachting.

Below Immaculately attired, a sailor pushes off one of *Britannia's* barges from the Royal Yacht Squadron steps. Only members of the club, officers of the Royal Navy and royalty may land at the squadron steps.

Right Naval ratings paint *Britannia's* anchor chain while other members of the crew sweep past in a whaler, or activity boat.

Below The paddle steamer *Embassy* – a familiar sight in the 1960s running mostly from Bournemouth to Totland Bay, or Yarmouth. During Cowes Week she usually made a couple of trips to view the Royal Yacht. Launched in 1911 *Embassy* was taken out of service in September 1966 and scrapped the following year.

Four generations at Cowes.

Above Crowds near the Royal Yacht Squadron strain their necks to watch the racing.

Opposite page top The 1960s comes to Cowes. Young people in mini skirts, colourful shirts and long hair.

Lower left Wet weather

Lower right A baby in a pram enjoys the sunshine on the Victoria Parade while *Britannia* rides at anchor in the background.

Above Waves wash ashore at the Royal Yacht Squadron during stormy weather.

Left Youngsters on the Victoria Parade enjoy the activity on the water during Cowes Week.

Above and right Hardy spectators brave the rain on Prince's Green to watch the regatta, or enjoy it from near the Royal Yacht Squadron when the sun puts in an appearance.

Above An inflatable rescue craft on the waterfront.

Left An American classic – an International One Design – sails past Uffa Fox's house on the left, and the Island Sailing Club and 18th-century Customs Watch House on the right. The yacht was designed in the 1930s by legendary yachtsman Cornelius Shields.

Below The Island Sailing Club, Globe hotel and Victoria Parade from the mouth of the River Medina.

Right Britain's most famous marine photographer, Keith Beken, at work in the Solent. The wooden camera was so heavy he needed both hands to hold it steady and had to release the shutter by biting a rubber bulb in his mouth.

Below Beken of Cowes – the marine photographer's shop in Birmingham Road, Cowes. The business was started by Frank Beken, who first took photographs of racing yachts in the 1890s.

Below right Father and son – Keith and Kenneth Beken – surrounded by nautical photos in their Cowes showroom.

An 18th-century sail-maker's loft seen from the Red Funnel walkway, Cowes. Restored in 1947 it became the Cowes home of the newspaper magnate, World War II fighter pilot and MP, Sir Max Aitken. When he died in 1985 Sir Max's home was converted into a maritime museum dedicated to his memory.

Right Crowded with passengers the Red Funnel car ferry *Osborne Castle* enters Cowes. At the height of the season this, and other vessels, provided an hourly service for the 12-mile trip. The *Osborne Castle* was 191 feet long and could carry 673 passengers and 25 cars. The ship was launched in 1962 and sold to a Canadian ferry company in 1978.

Below One of the great survivors, the *Balmoral,* comes into berth at the Red Funnel terminal – the Fountain pontoon – in Cowes. After she was launched in 1949 the ship served as a ferry between Southampton and Cowes before making her name cruising around the Isle of Wight. Red Funnel sold *Balmoral* in 1969, but she continued cruising elsewhere in Britain. The ship was still going strong in the new millennium.

Opposite page The dinghy quay. In the background is Lallow's boatyard, birthplace of many famous yachts.

Right Clouds gather over a busy Cowes harbour.

Below Two young fishermen hurry down to the waterfront in East Cowes. East Cowes was once the industrial heart of the Island. Here shipbuilders J. Samuel White and Saunders-Roe built high-speed ships, seaplanes and flying boats before World War II. The hovercraft was also developed here.

Left A Folkboat sails past Gurnard Bay while swimmers enjoy the sunshine. This small yacht was designed in Sweden in the 1940s as a people's boat. Cheap, fast and easy to sail, the sloop can be used for racing and family cruising at weekends. Thousands have been built. It is only 25 feet long and has a small cabin with two bunks. 'If you want to stand up,' said Uffa Fox, 'go on deck.'

Below Youngsters enjoy swimming off a bathing raft in Gurnard Bay, the sheltered seaside village to the west of Cowes. Here is the council's chief bathing place with safe bathing at all states of the tide. Visitors can hire a day hut, enjoy refreshments, a putting green and a holiday camp.

Opposite page top A giant Princess flying-boat mothballed in East Cowes. Saunders-Roe built three prototypes and the maiden flight took place in 1952. The Princess was one of the largest aircraft of its day. It had ten engines, a wing span of 219 feet and was meant to carry 105 passengers across the Atlantic in considerable comfort on two decks. But flying boats fell out of favour and the Princesses were broken up in 1967.

Opposite page bottom An elegant yacht rides at anchor in Cowes as evening draws on.

Left A teenager applauds the world's fastest liner, the *SS United States*, as she steams past Cowes and sets out for New York. Her knife-like bow and special design meant she could travel at 43 knots full speed ahead and over 20 knots in reverse. The American super-liner was 990 feet long and could carry 2,000 passengers and 1,000 crew. The *United States* was launched in 1952, and constructed of non-inflammable material. The owners boasted the only wood on board the ship was found in the pianos and butchers' blocks. Today the *United States* is moored in Philadelphia, her future uncertain.

Opposite page One of the highlights for holiday-makers was going out in a tourist boat to see the world's largest liner, *Queen Elizabeth* (83,000 tonnes), passing by in the Solent. The Cunarder was 1,031 feet long, carried 2,283 passengers and over 1,000 crew, and sped across the Atlantic to New York at 28.5 knots. The liner entered service in 1940 and retired in 1968. She was destroyed by fire in Hong Kong Harbour and sank in 1972.

Below The world's second largest liner, the *Queen Mary*, sweeps past the Island. She and her sister ship, *Queen Elizabeth*, dominated the transatlantic passenger trade from the late 1940s until the 1950s. They provided a two-ship weekly express service from Southampton to Cherbourg, then New York. Today the *Queen Mary* is a floating hotel in Long Beach, California.

Above Queen Victoria's favourite home, Osborne House in East Cowes, was partly designed by her husband, the Prince Consort. Its Italianate design was much copied elsewhere on the Island.

Below When James Wyatt built Norris Castle, in East Cowes, in 1799 he looked back to the Normans for inspiration. The result – a romantic building on the banks of the Solent with splendid views of the sea. Queen Victoria came to the castle as a young girl, fell in love with the Island and returned as queen to live next door at Osborne. The German Kaiser Wilhelm II also stayed here.

Above The royal church – St Mildred's, Whippingham, designed in a fairy-tale style by the Prince Consort. The parents of Earl Mountbatten are buried in the graveyard as well as the yacht designer Uffa Fox.

Newport & the River Medina

Opposite page The Guildhall, where law courts were once quartered, dominates Newport High Street. It was built in 1814-16 and designed by the Regency architect John Nash, who designed Buckingham Palace.

Left St Thomas Church and Square in the centre of Newport. Elderly people relax in the late afternoon sun in what was once the corn market for Tudor Newport. Centuries later the corn market moved to St James's Square. Princess Elizabeth of England, the daughter of Charles I, is buried inside the Victorian parish church.

Below left God's Providence House, with its beautiful 18th-century shell porch, stands on the site of an older house that was spared the plague in 1584. It is now a restaurant.

Newport Harbour. In 1977 the abandoned warehouses in the
background were converted into the thriving Quay Arts Centre,
with its gallery space, theatre and café.

The railway viaduct carried trains across Newport Harbour to the station. Both the station and the viaduct were demolished in 1973 to make way for the Newport relief road, now called Medina Way.

The port was just clinging on to commercial life when I photographed it during the 1960s.

The two photographs on this page are of the Harbour and Town Quay area.

The photographs on the opposite page show (*top*) a floating crane and a small coaster unloading, and (*bottom*) the aptly-named coaster *Needles* tied up at the Town Quay.

The area developed in the 16th and 17th centuries as the town grew in importance as a port. Stone-built quays and wharfs were added on both sides of the river where the Medina and Lukely Brook merged. By the middle of the 19th century the quay was encircled by warehouses.

Opposite page Evening at Newport Town Quay looking downstream towards the Model Stores and its electric derrick at Little London.

Right The Thames barge *Centaur* tied up at Newport quay.

Below Centaur's skipper, Tommy Baker, and the ship's dog.

Left A boatyard in Little London, Newport. An Austin A35 Countryman estate car is parked beside the boat drawn up on the hard.

Below left An old warehouse and gas lamp seen through a railway arch at Newport Harbour.

Below Little London seen across the River Medina, Newport.

Opposite page The once busy, but now derelict, Newport Station. The station was the Island's railway hub, with links to Yarmouth and Freshwater as well as Cowes, Ryde, Ventnor, Shanklin, Sandown and Bembridge, and the villages in between. The station closed in 1966 and was demolished in 1973. The site is now occupied by part of Medina Way.

Left Many of the Island's steam locomotives ended up like this at Newport Station after the closure of the lines.

Below One of the Island's steam locomotives awaits destruction.

Right A dog out for an evening run trots along the bank of the River Medina and over the remains of the East Medina tide mill sluice gate.

Below The remains of the East Medina tide mill showing the cast iron pit wheel and water wheel. Steam rises from Cowes power station on the horizon. The mill was built in the 19th century to mill corn, reputedly to supply ships transporting convicts from Southampton to Australia. The timber-built mill was gutted by fire during a bombing raid in the Second World War.

Above The Heroine of Dunkirk – the paddle steamer *Medway Queen* moored in the millpond at Binstead. The ship was launched in 1924, winning immortality when as one of the armada of 'little ships' she rescued 7,000 men from the beaches of Dunkirk in 1940. The *Medway Queen* was taken out of service in 1963, becoming a nightclub on the Isle of Wight. Later she was wrecked and eventually towed away to the mainland for restoration.

Right The new yacht marina under construction on the site of the old East Medina tide mill, Binstead.

Below The coal-fired paddle steamer *Kingswear Castle* was moored for a time at Binstead on the River Medina.

Wootton & Quarr

Wootton Bridge.

Above Wootton Bridge village lies a mile inland from the Solent at the end of Wootton Creek, midway between Ryde and Newport.

Right The late 18th-century Sloop Inn in Mill Square stood next door to the tide mill and was originally the miller's house. The mill itself was demolished in 1962.

Below Straw hats and colourful summer dresses are *de rigueur* for those in charge of the church fête stalls.

Above Members of the Salvation Army relax on the lawn during the 1965 Wootton Church Fête.

Opposite page Top The Governor of the Island, Earl Mountbatten of Burma, jokes as he opens the fête held in the garden of Wootton Lodge. At his side the rector, the Rev A.H. Genower, and the broadcaster and former approved school headmaster C.A. Joyce.

Bottom left The rector's granddaughter, Sheila Featherstone, curtsies as she presents a rosebud buttonhole to the Governor.

Bottom right The Governor pats a baby in its pram.

A band of Junior Guardsman played throughout the fête.

Left Young ice-cream eaters enjoy themselves at the fête.

Below left Playing skittles could win you a crate of beer.

Below Lost in thought amid all the bustle and excitement of the fête.

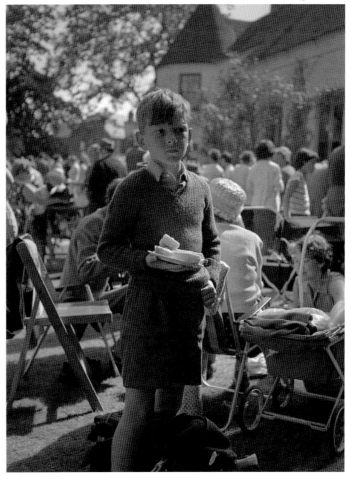

Above Some of the remains of the original Quarr Abbey founded in 1132 on the north coast near Wootton Creek. This farmhouse was built out of stone saved from the medieval building destroyed by Henry VIII.

Left The author explores the ruins of the original Quarr Abbey.

A side aisle in the abbey chapel.

Evening at Quarr Abbey showing the chapel and bell tower. This remarkable building, which was built entirely of rough Flemish bricks in 1911-12, was designed by the French Benedictine monk Dom Paul Bellot. His work astonished the architectural historian, Sir Nicholas Pevsner, who described Bellot as 'a virtuoso in brick' and 'one of the pioneers of 20th-century Expressionism.' Quarr Abbey was just one of Bellot's many buildings.

This and the Opposite page.
Inside Quarr Abbey. The abbey is largely self-supporting. The monks grow their own food and divide their time between worship, study, work and recreation. I took all of these photographs on a visit to the abbey in 1967. They show a monk in the pottery, the library, weaving, working a lathe and the kitchen. Carpentry, bookbinding and tailoring are also important.

Left   While two people dig for bait at Fishbourne, the British Rail car ferry *M.V. Fishbourne* arrives from Portsmouth. *Fishbourne* entered service in 1961 and carried 34 cars and 165 passengers at 10½ knots across the Solent. The six-mile journey took 45 minutes. The ferry service from Portsmouth to Fishbourne started in 1926 and since the early days has expanded to become a major force in transport to the Island.

Below   A boathouse at Fishbourne on the eastern bank of Wootton Creek.

Opposite page   The most famous view on the Island – the church and thatched cottages, Godshill. The present church dates from the early 14th century.

Heart of the Island

Left A battery of small cannon guard Carisbrooke Castle courtyard. In the centre is the Chapel of St Nicholas. The castle was once the residence of the Island Governor. Charles I was imprisoned here for a year before being taken to London for execution in 1649.

Below Godshill churchyard seen through the church entrance.

Below left Children feed the ducks in Lukely Brook, Carisbrooke.

Opposite page The tower of St Mary's Church, Carisbrooke, visible from Castle Street and Lukely Brook.

Above   A countryman trudges along a dusty lane in Carisbrooke.

Left   The Bridal steps of St Mary's Church lead down to Carisbrooke High Street.

Right The future prime minister, James Callaghan, was guest of honour at the Carisbrooke Cottage Garden Society's annual summer show in August 1965.

Below An Island policeman examines prize-winning vegetables.

Left   Mr Callaghan casts an expert eye over the runner beans.

Below   An elderly lady seems lost amid the hubbub.

Opposite page   Islanders play bingo with bottle tops.

Below Mr Callaghan pauses to sign an autograph while two Island policemen keep a genial eye on the proceedings.

What today seem a wonderfully old-fashioned variety of games give pleasure to young and old at the Carisbrooke Show.

A young boy tries to trace the shape of the Island with a metal ring
without touching the outline.

Above A steam train puffs through the countryside. The Island once boasted 54 miles of railways linking all the major towns, but most of the lines closed between 1952 and 1966, leaving only one from Ryde to Sandown and Shanklin and a heritage line run by volunteers.

Left A locomotive lets off steam at Havenstreet – one end of the Isle of Wight railway heritage line. Trains run for five miles to Wootton. The Isle of Wight Steam Railway was set up in 1971 and is one of the Island's most popular tourist attractions.

Opposite page A Royal Mail van waits outside the post office, Brighstone, in the south of the Island. Thatched cottages, tea gardens and a church form the heart of the old village.

Above A Ford Cortina speeds down a country road in the heart of the Island on a hot summer's afternoon.

Left Buses stuck in a country lane. Many of the Island roads are narrow and incidents such as this still occasionally happen.

Right A countryman with a scythe pauses from his work on a hot summer's afternoon.

Below A farmer ploughs a field at Calbourne in high summer. Nearly 74 per cent of the Isle of Wight's land is used for agriculture, horticulture, or forestry. The island is largely self-sufficient and exports food.

Above Sheat Manor, a beautiful Elizabethan building in the traditional E-shape, at the foot of Chillerton Down.

Right The ruined Appuldurcombe House. Begun in 1701 by Sir Robert Worsley the house was one of the grandest in the Island with grounds landscaped by Capability Brown. During the Second World War this elegant building was wrecked by a land mine. Only the burnt-out shell remained. This picture shows the house before it was re-roofed and the windows replaced giving the illusion that the building is still intact.

Opposite page A windswept tree high up on the Downs.

Sketching at Winkle Street, Calbourne. One of the prettiest and
most unspoilt villages on the Island.

Once called Barrington Row after a family who owned most of the village, Winkle Street at Calbourne is a popular tourist haunt. This attractive row of tiled and thatched cottages overlooks a small stream that drives the nearby water mill.

Set in 10 acres of countryside, Calbourne Water Mill is one of the oldest working mills in the country, dating back to the 17th century. There has been a mill on the site for a thousand years and the pond that provides water to turn the wheel existed in Domesday times. The mill produces about 30-40 tons of flour each year, supplying many island shops. It also delivers flour to the mainland and sells bags of flour and bread direct to customers. The photograph above is of the miller, Ronald Weeks, with the mill's original charter, and the one of the interior shows the roller units installed in 1893 to mill faster than traditional stones.

Opposite page   Ryde pier at sunset in the final days of steam.

Ryde & the East

Above   The paddle steamer *Sandown* approaches Ryde pier – the gateway to the Island. *Sandown* was built in 1934 for south coast excursions and used as a ferry from Portsmouth to Ryde. The paddle steamer was withdrawn from service in September 1965 and scrapped.

Left   Boys fishing for crabs on Ryde pier. Before the pier opened in 1814 visitors to Ryde had to trudge across half a mile of wet sand, or be carried on a porter's back, to reach the town. There are, in fact, three piers – the old one shown here for pedestrians, the tramway pier, and the railway or iron pier with stations at both ends.

Right Fly posters of Ryde pier advertise 1960s pop groups Amen Corner and the then largely unknown Pink Floyd.

Below The electric tram station at the end of Ryde pier. Originally horse-drawn trams transported passengers from the pier-head to the mainland when this second pier opened in 1864 alongside the pedestrian pier, but the horses were eventually replaced by an electric tramway.

Left Framed by coaches elderly people relax on the sea wall at Ryde.

Below Bowls and tennis courts in the Ryde Esplanade Gardens. Beyond lies the Pavilion where a theatrical company used to perform daily, a small bandstand and what the Red Guide called 'several tasteful shelters.'

Opposite page top A couple watch an evening game of cricket on Ryde sands.

Opposite page bottom Digging for bait on Ryde sands.

Above left An SRN6 hovercraft races into Ryde from Southsea. The SRN6 was designed to ferry 38 passengers, or 3 tonnes of freight, at high speed across sheltered waters. Brought into service in 1965 it travelled at an average speed of 30-35 knots, but could reach 52 knots. People complained about the noise generated by the gas turbine engine. In addition, the rotating tips of the propeller created a noise like angry wasps as they broke the sound barrier.

Above Passengers emerge from the bow of an SRN6 hovercraft at Ryde.

Left As an SRN6 hovercraft lumbers ashore at Ryde a member of the ground crew leaps on board to wrench open the door so passengers can disembark.

Opposite page Amid clouds of sand and spray an early hovercraft – the Westland SRN2 – takes off from Ryde and flies across the Solent on a cushion of air. In the summer of 1963 Hovertransport ran an experimental passenger service between Southsea and Ryde coming ashore on Appley Beach. The SRN2 was 65 feet long and could carry over 50 passengers.

Above Sailors from the Seaview Yacht Club row ashore with their gear after sailing in their Seaview One Design dinghies moored out in the harbour.

Right Seaview Yacht Club. Wooden rowing boats line the shore while yacht races are organised by a race officer and officials from the race deck opposite the start line. Established in 1893, the club is unusual in owning a fleet of racing keelboats – the Seaview Mermaids. It is also the home for a fleet of clinker-built dinghies – the Seaview One Designs.

Opposite page Small boats drawn up on the High Street Slip, Seaview. The maritime village is situated on a prominent headland at the north-eastern extremity of the Island. With its narrow streets and alleyways sloping down to the water Seaview retains much of its Victorian and Edwardian charm.

Left The old tidal mill, St Helens. The mill and mill dam were built in 1780 and its pair of tide-driven wheels drove eight sets of grinding stones. Much of its corn was shipped in by sea by barges. In due course, Edward Way and Sons became the working owners, along with the Isle of Wight Farmers Trading Society. They operated until the mill's closure in 1931. The building was demolished in 1969 and a private house built on the site. The dam, now known as the Causeway, remains intact and forms part of the Island's coastal path.

Below Bembridge Sailing Club, a traditional sailing club formed in 1886. The period clubhouse with a clock tower adds an elegant note to activities on the water and enhances the harbour scene.

Opposite page Bembridge Harbour – man-made and constructed in the latter part of the 19th century – is always crowded with yacht and small boats – though those in my 1960s photograph evoke a very different world of yachting to those in the Harbour today.

Above Bembridge's early 18th century windmill is the only windmill to survive on the Island. The mill last operated in 1913. During the Second World War it was used by the Home Guard as an observation post. Such were the acoustics that people inside the mill could hear enemy aircraft approaching ten minutes before the warning sirens sounded.

Left Much of the original wooden machinery survives inside Bembridge Windmill.

Opposite page Watcombe and Compton Bays, Freshwater, on a summer's afternoon.

West Wight

Above The 38-foot high granite cross on the High Down, Freshwater, erected in 1897 to Tennyson's memory.

Left Tennyson's Bridge links Farringford with the High Down. Such was the poet's fame, that Tennyson used to run across it to avoid the admirers gathered below.

Below Farringford House, now an hotel, was the home of Alfred Lord Tennyson for 40 years.

Solent sentinel – the Needles Lighthouse – 102 feet high and
visible for 17 miles. Set in the western approaches at the extreme
western end of the Island, the chalk stacks are a hazard to ships
making their way up the Solent to Portsmouth and Southampton
Water. The present lighthouse was built in 1859. It looks very
different today to when I photographed it in 1965, as there is now
a helicopter pad on the summit.

Above The famous Arch Rock at Freshwater Bay was destroyed by heavy seas in the early 1990s.

Left Holidaymakers go on board small boats from Alum Bay, famous for its coloured cliffs, with the Needles on the horizon.

Below The path that leads from the Green Gate on the Farringford estate up to Tennyson Down.

Opposite page Two photographs showing the view from Tennyson Down looking east towards Freshwater and Compton Bays.

Left Fishing off the sea wall at Freshwater Bay.

Below Cows graze in front of the elegant King's Manor Farm, Freshwater.

All Saints, Freshwater, one of the oldest churches on the island dating back to the Domesday survey. The 13th-century tower looks down on the village street. Tennyson and his family worshipped here and memorials recall their association.

Below Yarmouth Tide Mill, built in 1793 to meet the rising demand for flour during the wars with France. One hundred years later the nearby railway reduced the water supply to the tidal pond and the mill declined. The machinery was removed, the mill became a private home and the historian A.J.P. Taylor lived here.

Opposite page The Square, Yarmouth, on a hot summer's afternoon showing the Bugle Hotel and St James's church.

Above Yarmouth Harbour.

Left The car ferry *Freshwater* arrives at Yarmouth from Lymington on the mainland. Launched in 1959 the *Freshwater* carried 26 cars and 560 passengers. An expensive Daimler comes off the ship, followed by an inexpensive symbol of the 1960s, a Mini.

Opposite page Yarmouth Harbour on a summer's afternoon. The lifeboat is moored behind the small sailing dinghy and the car ferry has docked.

Above Good fishing can be had off Yarmouth's 700-feet long Victorian wooden pier. On the left is the Royal Solent Yacht Club founded in 1878. The clubhouse was designed by Sir Aston Webb who designed the Queen Victoria memorial in front of Buckingham Palace and the Admiralty Arch at the end of the Mall.

Opposite page Steephill Cove lies a mile west of Ventnor. As well as the sandy beach, there are a handful of cottages and cafés.

Below Yarmouth pier seen from the waiting-room.

Holiday Coast

Left Elegant Victorian houses decorate the Ventnor seafront.

Below The ironmongers W. Hurst and Son, High Street, Ventnor. A Victorian ironmongers founded in Newport in 1859 and still going strong 150 years later. The firm gradually expanded across the Island, including Ventnor in the 1960s.

Opposite page Ventnor - the pearl of the southern coast – lies on the slopes of a steep hill nearly 800 feet high. The resort has a Mediterranean feel. Originally a fishing village, the town grew up as a health resort in Victorian times after the eminent physician, Sir James Clark, recommended the mild climate. He said it was ideal for the treatment of pulmonary diseases. Tuberculosis was then rife, and sufferers flocked to Ventnor from all over Britain. The seaside town rapidly developed from a few cottages into a fashionable holiday resort. In about 30 years the population swelled from 800 to 5,000.

Right A steep road zigzags down to Ventnor's Esplanade past the Cascade.

Below Ventnor is carved out of the side of the cliff in a series of terraces, with long flights of steps and 1 in 4 gradients in some streets. The picture shows the junction of four roads – Ocean View Road, Mitchell Avenue, Grove Road and South Grove Road. Here was the entrance to Ventnor Station, which closed in the 1960s and became an industrial estate. The building on the left is the Terminus public house. The building with the spire was originally the Ventnor Water Company. This supplied untreated spring water from the chalky downs above Ventnor to a local brewery as it was ideal for beer-making.

Opposite page The derelict Ventnor Station – one of two that once linked the coastal town to the rest of the Island and brought holidaymakers flooding in.

Above A double-decker bus struggles up the Undercliff road towards Ventnor. On the left is the sea, on the right a cliff 200 feet high.

Right Horse riders trot past Pelham Woods in the Undercliff, near Ventnor.

Opposite page Ventnor from Ventnor Park. In the distance is the Victorian pier, which was demolished in 1993 having been wrecked by storms and fallen into disrepair.

Above St Catherine's Oratory on St Catherine's Down dates to the 14th century. A priest kept a light burning to guide shipping rounding the headland.

Above right St Catherine's Lighthouse was built in 1838 to replace an earlier lighthouse which stood on higher ground, but which was often shrouded in fog. The light from the 86 feet high tower is visible for 17 miles.

Right The electric lamp bulb in St Catherine's Lighthouse generates 6,000,000 candle power when magnified by powerful lenses.

Opposite page Two views of the southern coast. The top one looks west towards Ventnor, the lower shows a small cove near St Lawrence.

Above Which way should we go? A coastal sign points the way to Ventnor, Wroxall and Shanklin. Or the keen hiker might make for the interior of the Island and the rolling downland in the background.

Left Pictures of the Old Village, Shanklin, adorn countless calendars and chocolate boxes. The thatched roofs, quaint shop fronts and Crab Hotel still delight visitors. The entrance to the chine is to the right of the hotel in the centre of the picture.

Opposite page Shanklin Pier opened in 1891 and was 1200 feet long. It was bombed during the Second World War and fuel pipes used for the PLUTO project ran from the pier across the English Channel. After the war the pier staged entertainments for holidaymakers during the season. But in October 1987 the worst storm in 200 years hit southern England. Shanklin Pier was ripped apart and destroyed.

Above Sandown, the sister resort of Shanklin, sits in the centre of Sandown Bay. Sandown's pier is the only Victorian pier on the south coast to survive into the new millennium.

Opposite page The isolated Fleetlands Farm, Shalfleet.

Below A family enjoy a stroll along Culver Cliff overlooking Sandown Bay. Sandown pier can be glimpsed two and half miles away through the summer haze.

A Quiet Corner

The church of St. Michael the Archangel, Shalfleet. The Norman tower, which resembles a fort, dates from the 11th century and the walls are five feet thick. During the French invasions it formed a place of refuge for the local population. A 3-pounder gun was kept at its base to fight off marauders.

Shalfleet viewed from the top of the church tower. The village – complete with a church, manor, inn and cottages – grew up around a crossroads on the flat northern shore where the Caul Bourne widens into a creek.

Above A town hall with no town. Located in the quiet village of Newtown on the edge of a marshland nature reserve this 17th-century building was once at the centre of a small town. Newtown was attacked by the French in 1377 and in later centuries the harbour silted up. Despite its decline Newtown was represented by two members of Parliament until 1832. These included John Churchill, later first Duke of Marlborough; and George Canning who became Prime Minister. The Town Hall is now the only remaining monument to Newtown's past glories.

Right The boathouse at the end of the world, or so it feels. Newtown Quay, surrounded by marshes, is largely deserted and unspoilt. Plans to build a nuclear power station in the area were resisted by local people.

The gaff cutter *Laura* tied up at Newtown Quay, with Gull Island in the background. Launched in 1900, *Laura* was still sailing over 100 years later during which time she had only three owners. One was Mr. Atkey, the chandler in Cowes – the business still trades under his name. He used *Laura* to run supplies back and forth from the mainland.

The author at the time he started photographing the Isle of Wight.

THE PHOTOGRAPHS

Most of the pictures in this book were taken with a Rolleicord Vb camera. This took 12 photos on 6x6 cm film. The Rolleicord had a simple four-element f3.5 Schneider lens, but this was surprisingly sharp. It could produce giant prints, or enabled you to enlarge a tiny segment of the negative and produce a sharp picture. I used a medium speed black and white film – Kodak Verichrome Pan, though I experimented with others, including colour.

When I first started I was influenced by the pictures in *Country Life* magazine, and the work of the travel photographer J. Allan Cash. Allan used a Rolleiflex and insisted on technical perfection. He abhorred grain and blur. He preferred taking pictures in bright sunlight and used filters to bring out the clouds. So did I.

The American landscape photographer Ansel Adams also influenced me. He, too, favoured strong sunlight and used a red filter to darken the sky almost to black. His rhetorical way of seeing seeped into my work. You can see his influence in my pictures of the Needles lighthouse, *Britannia* and the Cunard liners.

I also bought a second-hand Leica with a 28mm wide-angle lens and used this for a few shots. When I returned to the island in later years I used an Olympus 35mm camera.